Here I Stand

Devon Grasley

BookLeaf Publishing

Presentation by *BookLeaf Publishing*

Web: www.bookleafpub.com

E-mail: info@bookleafpub.com

ISBN: 9789357213318

First edition 2023

Dysmorphia

Looking in the mirror
More lost than ever
Desiring a thinner body
Afraid to eat
Afraid to move
My own self worth
So low it's paralyzing
I see few traces of
Who I once was
The girl who seemingly has it all together
Falling apart in front of her very own eyes

Worst Addiction

Your lips on mine
More intoxicating than any blacked out Friday
More addicting than chasing the first high
Craving you is my worst habit
Needing you is my shameful desire
    -You are my worst addiction

Cynical Love

I used to believe in fairytale endings
And red roses and white dresses
But now most of the songs I sing are sad
And the words I write represent
The shattered pieces of what's left of me
I'm a girl who had her heart shattered
Just one too many times
To believe in a happy ever after
I'm now just a lost hopeless romantic
Caught up in the world's cynical love story

Life Support

I would have loved you with a love
that heals all the scars
If only I had loved myself first
and my own scars
were the downfall I never saw coming
Internally bleeding out
until the love I could have given you faded out
like the light in my eyes
I never wanted you to be my life support
I never wanted you to be the one to pull the plug

Drowning

You were the air my lungs were craving
You were also the reason I was drowning

Always a second choice

So at the end of the day
I'll change into the PJs you bought me
and the shirt that holds your faintest scent
I'll pull it as close to me as possible
and pretend
that when I slip into my dreams
I'll find your arms once again around me
Until the morning comes
and I remember
I'm not the one you want to hold
I'm the one you chose to let go.

The Mask of Depression

Depression isn't always scars on wrists
Or skin and bones
It's not always the "sadness" that drowns
Its the pressure on your chest that only you notice
Its the smile on your face you have to force
It's the heavy mind mixed with light conversation
Its the reminder of every loss you ever had suddenly crashing your late afternoon coffee date with a friend
Just because my face has no tears
That doesn't mean my soul isn't crying
It's bringing you to the edge of insanity
And secretly wishing you could jump off
But for you ill paint a smile
I'll laugh a little and live a little
While slowly dying inside.

Shell

You Fell in love with
The way your hands
felt on my body
and not the way my heartbeats
So forgive me when you say "I miss you"
and I remind you that it was never me you
missed
You simply missed the shell of me.

Passing By

Lifes a blur
Full of mesmerizing colors
I can't comprehend
A rush of wind as time passes by
And I'm always on the outside looking in

Letting Go

I'm afraid to stop missing you
Afraid to move on
Even though we never were
We could've been
And moving on
Means letting go of the possibility
Means letting go of the what-ifs
Means letting go of you
-And I'm not ready to let go of you just yet
-You may still come back

Retribution

I am not responsible for how I chose to heal
What you shattered
I am not responsible for the way I picked up the pieces
You left me shattered with
And I sure am not responsible for the pain you feel
Now that you finally realize
I'm gone

Self-Love

So I lay awake at night
And wonder
If all the choices
All the hard work
The battles I've lost
In an attempt to win this war
All the scars that now paint my body
I wonder
If who I am is worth the pain
How can I expect anyone to love me
If I still look in the mirror and turn away
"Do I even love me?"

Misery

Misery
They say misery love company
And through your eyes
I'm walking with a target on my back
I'm so sick of being the person you force to
share your misery with

Nightmares

I'm terrified to fall asleep
But the sad truth is
The demons in my dreams
Are far more kind
Then the ones I face
When I'm awake

Your Loss

I'm the girl who would give everything to you
All my love
My heart
My affections
Id write a million poems
And a thousand books all for you
But at the end of the day
I wont let my love go to waste
I just hope you know
You lost the girl who would have given you
everything

Beautiful Love

You were never part of my plan
But here you are
Breaking down all my walls
Brick by brick
And i'm finding it easier to let you in
Knowing very well my heart will be broken
But thats what falling in love is like
Its slow
Its agonizingly painful
Yet breathtakingly beautiful

You Lost me

You didn't lose someone who didn't care
Not a girl who'd drive off and never look back
But a girl who would constantly give up her
world
Turn around at every red light
Just for the chance to pull into your drive one
last time
You lost a girl who'd stop the world and bring
you the moon
You didn't lose a nobody
You lost me

The Heart of a Warrior

Your scars are beautiful love
They show that even after
the world has beat you down
And torn you to shreds
You are still standing
You can endure the cold hands of the world
and still be here today
Even on days where your mind is just as broken
as your body
You still take a few steps forward
That is a strength found within
Your scars are outwardly reminders of who you
are on the inside
You have the Heart of a Warrior

Reflection

Even as the pink skies meet the crystal water
Creating a sunset dream
I too can find beauty in my reflection
And so can you

Changes

Like autumn leaves fall
My love for you is slowly starting to change
And eventually
I'll drift off with a fading breeze
Leaving me naked and bare
With nothing but a chance to bloom
Into something beautiful

Life Vest

For when you are lost at sea
and drowning in the waves of sorrow
I will wrap my arms around you
and float us back to shore
I will be your life vest through stormy waters

www.ingramcontent.com/pod-product-compliance
Lightning Source LLC
Chambersburg PA
CBHW051722130826
49812CB00034B/1308
9789357213318

Green Strawberries

Anna Green

BookLeaf Publishing

Presentation by *BookLeaf Publishing*

Web: www.bookleafpub.com

E-mail: info@bookleafpub.com

ISBN: 9789357445955

First edition 2023

Conspicuous Markers

Conspicuous markers of a painful past invite
questions from curious, well-meaning friends
and acquaintances.

Self-harm scars, a parent who has passed, gaps
in education, always missing class.

A criminal record spent but always lasts, and
four separate primary schools, racked up good
and fast.

Sleeves in the summer? That mark on your arm?
Why so many primary schools, did it do harm?

When did your dad die? How is your mum? And
why, when I mention her, do you look glum?

Now cough up a light-hearted reply
To a question on something you strongly deny
My dad's not dead,
I went to one school,
And never drove teachers right up the wall

Make it digestible, don't share too much. Hide all your pain which is hot to the touch. You can't just start crying, here in this shop, people will think that you've lost the plot. Well maybe I have, for all I know, is that hiding the pain has caused it to grow. In the absence of shame, who might I be? Take a step forward and you might just see.

Motherly Love

Motherly Love
You are safe now, put down your guard
You can relax, although it is hard
You are kind, good, and eternally loving
With so much to give, and so much coming
Open up to the possibility
That staying sad is not how it should be
No need to explain or justify why
It's taken this long to open your eyes
But here you are, sturdy and present
And rejection and abandonment are never pleasant
What happened was real, but can harm you no more
Because you have the tools
To stay grounded on the floor
And at the very least, you are fundamentally fine
With no hidden badness, that you need to hide
Just your humanity, show it with pride
Abandon your fears
And enjoy this life

Shame

Shame is the silent killer
Your cheeks blush pink, your heart rate increases
You compensate for the void within
By looking down your nose at someone else
Who is just living their life, like anybody else
But you cannot bear it
You cannot hide that you hate it so much
Your face feels warm
You look at yourself and all you have done; it all feels so wrong
You compensate for the burning shame
By complaining about how
Your colleague today, made a stupid comment
And it's all on them, and the blame's all theirs
But you are fantastic, like Beyonce or Rihanna
Because you cannot bear
The reality that you feel
That you are innately wrong, and there always will be
And your face burns pink
It let you down again,
Your hands start to shake
And you desperately look at the faces of others
for approval or assurance that you are enviably

talented and clever and pretty and worshipped
and revered
When all you need is to know that you matter,
and are loved

Anger

Picked tears
Rise up to the surface
Heart rate rises
Rash decisions
Are suddenly made
Anger is exhausting
That's why I suppress it
No wish to be seen
But grows beneath the light
Shine on your rage
And watch it dissipate
Not fester and bubble
Under the skin, so lift the lid
Release yourself
Swim to safety
Back to land
And after all
I am still me

Remnants

I sit at my dad's oak wood chest
His DNA still embedded
Somewhere in the cracks
I imagine
The clang of bin men
And I relish at the thought
Of even having a bin to change
I can't quite believe my luck

The Truth Can't Hurt

To be told of a morning
By someone unknown
That you sit on a spectrum
And are not alone
You knew all along
But acceptance was slow
Now befriend the truth
You saw long ago

Woman

The Divine Feminine
A circular Mound
Round as a pound
Up in the clouds
We shun our soft midriffs
Resent our red blood
Denied intuitions
Lost deep in the mud
But wisdom is held
In the Roundness of hips
In God's Own Green Earth
Pink, plump pouting lips
In flowing long lashes
Let's fill up our cups
Right to the brim
With a feminine touch

Proof

Proof that I am a woman
Proof I am a witch
Proof that I am good enough
Proof I am a bitch
No authentic response
Comes out of my brain
Just what the people want
And that is my domain

Tight

The tighter you cling
The harder they pull
Away
The very thing you crave
Is the very thing they have
But the way in which you seek it
Makes them hide away

Nonsense

The thought of you
Leaving for more
Brings me joy and pain
In equal measure
For love is not possessive
But it makes you want it all
A painful reminder
That I'm not as I once was
A cheerful truth faced
A double edged sword
Because the truth will set you free
But brings great shame all the same
How to break free
From a shameful truth
Look in the mirror
Breath deeply
Smile
And release

Enya

Dad borrowed the car to go to an Enya concert
But he did not come back
Now whenever I hear her voice
I yell, 'Turn off the track!'
For I cannot see
How Dad came to be
A candle in the wind
Overlooking the Irish sea
I hope he lives the rest of his days
Safe inside Manderley

Counting down

Counting down the seconds
Until I read Rebecca again
Going to order on Amazon
I give it 10/10

Surrender

Art connects you to a higher power
Something flows through you
And you must surrender
But when ego strikes
Your creativity
Falls to the wayside
It's about sales, outcome, approval, likes
Not the process

The Pull

Eyes locked in
A sudden urge
To reply to the messages
You thought were boring
Reaching out to friends, old and new
Lovers you want to forget
For the morning coffee
Is a driver of all things fantastic
But the aftermath bites you on the arse

White Forest

The price we pay for yesterday's sun
Is a foggy, frost-tipped morning
A welcome, white forest
Laid across the land

Inertia

The depletion of joy,
Unfolds with inertia
In direct, inverse correlation
Ego inflation
As compensation
For numbed emotion
Internal commotion

Goggins

As the old adage says
If you're not winning,
You're losing
If you're not growing
You deplete
Wither
Regress
Chug along, roll with the tides
Build every day like Lego
Small pieces forwards
And don't look back

Challenge

I want out of this challenge
Please no more

Interruption

To rudely interject
With a memory, thought or idea
Without waiting your turn
Has the opposite desired effect
Instead of being seen, being heard, and
understood
People just stare on bewildered
There's no harm in waiting
You're safe in the queue
Though malice is not
Behind the outbursts
It's a fear of forgetting
That drives going first
An untapped reaction
Without much care
Leads you to trigger
That bewildered stare

www.ingramcontent.com/pod-product-compliance
Lightning Source LLC
Chambersburg PA
CBHW051722130826
49812CB00034B/1307
* 9 7 8 9 3 5 7 4 4 5 9 5 5 *